TAKE BACK AMERICA

Mathew D. Staver

Foreword by Dr. Jerry Falwell

Liberty Counsel • Orlando, Florida

Take Back America

Copyright © 2000 Mathew D. Staver

Published by Liberty Counsel
          PO Box 540774
          Orlando, Florida 32854
          (407) 875-2100

Cover Design: Laura Sipple

First printing, 2000

Printed in the United States of America

Library of Congress Cataloging-in-Publication Data
Staver, Mathew D., 1956-
     Take Back America/Mathew D. Staver
          p.   cm.
     1. Church and state-United States. 2. Freedom of religion
- United States. 3. Religion in the public schools - Law and
legislation - United States. I. Title.
Library of Congress Card Number: 00-107778
ISBN 0-9662079-7-1

Table of Contents

Acknowledgments

Since 1992, I have preached the essence of this book in various churches around the country. It is my hope that the message contained herein educates and motivates you as it has me.

I would like to thank Candy McGuire for her diligence in typing this book. Despite a hectic schedule, Candy was able to bring this manuscript to print.

Annette Stanley patiently edited the final drafts. She has persevered to the end even when encountering portions of text that were not always compliant with her commands.

I would also like to thank Terri Litman for her diligence in coordinating my schedule. She has been able to juggle multiple tasks under stressful situations.

Laura Sipple has also juggled many jobs while still making time to design the book cover. I greatly appreciate her dedication to this project.

Finally, I would like to thank my wife, Anita. She has been able to manage my hectic schedule, work, and law school all at the same time. In the summer of 2000, she graduated from law school *summa cum laude* and received the honor of class valedictorian. Anita is not only my best friend, she is now my co-counsel.

Foreword

By Dr. Jerry Falwell

The very first time I met Mat Staver, I knew he was a man anointed by God for a very noble purpose: to protect and defend our constitutionally guaranteed religious freedoms.

Since forming Liberty Counsel in 1989 as a religious liberties education and legal defense organization, Mat has fulfilled his calling as a Christian attorney by defending our religious freedom with great success.

Mat has been instrumental in a number of landmark cases before state courts, federal courts and even the United States Supreme Court. He defends the First Amendment rights of adults and children who are accused of nothing more than the free expression of their deeply held spiritual beliefs and values.

Since 1998, Mat's Religious Freedom Report has been a featured segment of *Listen America*, my live weekly television talk program. In addition he writes a regular column dealing with religious freedom issues in my *National Liberty Journal* monthly newspaper.

With the publication of *Take Back America*, Mat has struck a blow for the restoration of our cherished Judeo-Christian values that in recent years have been the target of an intolerant irreligious minority.

It has become evident that we have neglected to maintain constant vigil over our religious freedoms. The withdrawal of faith-based citizens from the public square has emboldened the forces of darkness to declare that our values are no longer welcome. Now we face a tough fight to change the direction of our nation while we have the opportunity to do so.

America has forgotten its biblical roots. Children in public schools have in particular become targets of anti-Christian bigotry and legal terrorism under the guise of the so-called "separation of church and state," a practice Mat debunks as unconstitutional in itself.

Uncoupled from its biblical base, America has become a nation of uncurbed excesses. Night after night we see stories of violence and mayhem in our cities. Our schools have become war zones. Our entertainment serves to promote the basest impulses of society.

Such a time calls for people of God to once again turn to Him, instead of government, as the source of healing for our land. As Mat writes, "No form of government, republic or dictatorship, can restrain an unrestrained people."

The first step in taking back America is for Christians to take back their families. From that foundation we can strongly challenge the anti-God forces that have gripped our nation.

This well-documented and informative book is a valuable tool for parents, pastors, educators, business people and all citizens that care about the future of this great nation.

-DR. JERRY FALWELL,
Chancellor, Liberty University

Preface

In November of 1992, former Governor William Jefferson Clinton was elected as the forty-second President of the United States. As I searched for the reasons why someone of Mr. Clinton's "character" could become President of the United States, I realized that his rise to power was not the fault of Ross Perot diluting the popular vote, nor was the reason due to the politics of the Republican party. The answers were deeper, and the reasons were more complex.

I began reading the book of Deuteronomy. When I came to chapter 28, I was astounded. The entire chapter read like a daily newspaper. I had read this chapter many times before, but this time something was different.

The theme of Deuteronomy is simple: If you obey God and keep His commandments, the nation will be blessed; if you disobey God and His commandments, the nation will be cursed. The blessings and curses will affect every level of society, from the family to the farmer, from the city to the commander in-chief.

In addition to reading the book of Deuteronomy, I have spent a lot of time reading the Declaration of Independence. The Declaration of Independence has become my favorite historical document. I encourage everyone to read the Declaration several times a year. The Declaration clearly sets forth the founders' understanding of the purpose and role of government.

Our nation was founded upon Christian principles of morality and virtue. These great principles were not separated from religion. They were inspired and undergirded by religion. The founding fathers presupposed that the people would be virtuous and self-restrained. Virtue and self-restraint would flow from religious values. This is not to say that all the early settlers were Christian,

but they nevertheless operated from a general Christian or
religious world view.

Over the past several decades, our country has become
more and more secular. At the same time the country has
become more secular, the country has also become more
splintered. Chaos has replaced order. Fear has replaced
tranquility. In an effort to remedy the general breakdown
of our society and the rising crime rate, Americans seem
eager to give up their rights in exchange for a promise
from government to protect them. Our elected officials
promise more state and federal money, more programs,
more police. These efforts to remedy societal ills are like
putting a band-aid on cancer. While the band-aid might
appear to fix the problem, underneath the cancer continues
to spread.

The message of Deuteronomy is straightforward. No
amount of programs will put Humpty Dumpty back
together again. Humpty Dumpty must be fixed from
within. The founders understood this concept when they
penned the Declaration of Independence. This great
document is, in my opinion, the most powerful historical
document of America. The founders understood that the
Declaration was a "reflection of the American mind."
More than any other document, it declares the purpose of
government and the inspiration behind the American
Revolution.

It is my desire that this book will inspire you to reflect
on the message of Deuteronomy and the Declaration of
Independence. It is also my hope that you take seriously
our precious freedoms, and that the message of these two
great documents will motivate you to reclaim the values
and principals upon which this great country was founded.

-MATHEW D. STAVER, B.A., M.A., J.D.
President and General Counsel
Liberty Counsel

1

God Is The Foundation Of Government

God is the foundation of good government and national prosperity. Regardless of your religious belief or disbelief, any reasonable person must concede that America is broken. Violent crime plagues not only our inner cities but our public schools. Following the tragic shootings at Columbine High School in Littleton, Colorado,[1] even the secular talk show hosts acknowledged that all is not well with America. Something must be done.

Some have postulated that we need more federal money to put extra police officers on the streets and metal detectors in the schools. Some say more guidance counselors addressing violence or laws prohibiting hate speech will remedy the rampant violence. Others argue that we need prayer in our public schools. The answer you reach will in part be influenced by the history you know.

America doesn't need another program. Money won't fix our problems. Articulate politicians will not save us. We need God in America again. There is a clear biblical and historical basis for this proposition.

---

[1] On April 20, 1999, two boys, ages seventeen and eighteen, shot and killed twelve classmates and one teacher, wounding twenty-three others before killing themselves. Many of these shootings were religiously motivated. The gunmen asked some of the students whether they believed in Jesus, and when they said yes, the gunmen fired a bullet into their heads.

Biblical Basis

When the nation of Israel was on the verge of entering the Promised Land, Moses knew their future hung in a delicate balance. In order to prepare his people to take the land, he instructed them in the laws of God. The book of Deuteronomy is essentially the second giving of the law or a rehearsing of the law. Except for a few people, those entering the Promised Land were not part of the exodus from Egypt. These people were not around when God gave the Ten Commandments to Moses. Moses therefore instructed this young nation in the laws of God.

In chapter 28 of the book of Deuteronomy, God gives the children of Israel a choice. This is the chapter of the Blessings and the Curses. The choice is clear. The nation can choose to obey God and reap his blessings, or disobey God and incur the inevitable curses. There are two paths to choose. The first path is outlined in verses 1-14 and the second path is revealed in verses 15-68. The only difference in following one path as opposed to the other is how the nation corporately, and people individually, relate to God. If you accept God and follow His commands, then you will inevitably be blessed. On the contrary, if you reject God and His laws, you will reap the inevitable result of your choice.

When you purchase a car, you have a series of choices to make. You can follow the owner's manual to prolong the life of the car, or you can ignore the manufacturer's warnings and reap the consequences. If you drive your car without oil, the engine will inevitably blow. The manufacturer didn't cause the engine to blow. You did. The manufacturer gave you guidance on how to properly maintain the car. It is up to you to follow these rules or reject them. It is the same with the teachings of Deuteronomy. God simply reminds us of the inevitable result of our choice to reject Him.

The blessings portion of Deuteronomy 28 begins in verse 1.

> If you fully obey the Lord your God and carefully follow all His commands I give you today, the Lord your God will set you high above all the nations on earth.

If you obey God and follow His commands, then verse 3 says you will be blessed in the city. Verse 6 says, "You will be blessed when you come in and blessed when you go out." This verse pictures a city free of violence. The doors of the walled city are not shut. They remain open. There is no reason to shut them because there is no violence in or outside the city. You will be as safe and secure in the city as you will be when you travel outside the city.

Verses 4-5 say that you will be blessed in your gross national product. The production of goods, services and food will be plentiful. Verse 4 indicates that both animal and human reproduction will continue to be at peak levels.

> The fruit of your womb will be blessed, and the crops of your land and the young of your livestock -- calves of your herds and the lambs of your flocks.

Your basket and your kneading trough will be blessed.

Another consequence of following God and His commandments is that you will experience peace and security. You will not only have domestic security as indicated in verse 6, but you will have international security as outlined in verse 7. Chapter 28, verse 7, indicates that whenever an enemy will attack, the enemy will come in one way but be forced to flee in multiple directions. The military might will be unsurpassable by enemy nations.

The Lord will grant that the enemies who rise up against you will be defeated before you. They will come at you from one direction but flee from you in seven.

One of the blessings that flows from obeying God is abundant prosperity. Other people on earth will know that you serve the Lord. Corporately you will lend to many nations and not borrow. God finished instructing Moses regarding the blessings in verses 9-14:

The Lord will establish you as His holy people, as he promised you on oath, if you keep the commands of the Lord your God and walk in His ways. Then all the peoples on earth will see that you are called by the name of the Lord, and they will fear you. The Lord will grant you abundant prosperity -- in the fruit of your womb, the young of your livestock and the crops of your ground -- in the land he swore to your forefathers to give you.

The Lord will open the heavens, the storehouse of His bounty, to send rain on your land in season and to bless all the work of your hands. You will lend to many nations but will borrow from none. The Lord will make you the head, not the tail. If you pay attention to the commands of the Lord your God that I give you this day and carefully follow them, you will always be at the top, never at the bottom. Do not turn aside from any of His commands I give you today, to the right or to the left, following other gods and serving them.

However, Deuteronomy 28, verse 15, begins the curses. Verse 15 states that if you do not obey God, all of the curses will hunt you down and devour you corporately and individually.

If you disobey God, you will be cursed in your city. Verse 16 pictures a city in shambles, both morally and economically. In America today, we have cities which have gone bankrupt. One of the leading centers for murder is our nations's capital in Washington, D.C. Many cities no longer have sufficient funds to adequately staff their police forces. Many city streets are now paved with potholes.

Verses 17-18 say you will be cursed in your field. The production of goods and services will lag behind international competitors. Today our farmers are in trouble. Many farms are on the verge of collapse. We face a farming crisis in America because of the rising cost of farm equipment and the decreased amount of exports. Farms that have literally been in families for decades are on the verge of the auction block.

In verse 18, Deuteronomy states that a disobedient nation will experience infertility in both animals and humans. Today, millions of children have been slaughtered by abortion. Thousands of women have become sterile.

Chapter 28, verse 19, states that we will no longer have security if we reject God. I remember growing up as a little boy in a rural Florida town. We lived in a trailer without air conditioning. During the day we would leave the trailer door wide open. Never did we fear that an intruder would break into our home while we were there. When we went shopping at the local mall, we kept the windows down in our car and did not lock the doors. I remember many people leaving keys in their car. It was unheard of to have your car stolen. However, today we lock the doors during the day even though we are home. We install burglar alarms to guard our dwelling while we are absent and during the night. Hardly anyone leaves their car doors unlocked when they park the car in public. We even lock our car doors during the day when the car is parked in our driveway.

Verse 20 states that we will experience confusion if we reject God. Certainly we are confused today when we have to debate the most elementary topic of marriage. It should be obvious that marriage is confined to a lasting relationship between a man and a woman. However, when we have to debate today about same sex marriage, we have digressed in our thinking rather than advanced. We are confused in our reasoning.

Today we no longer have a platform from which we can argue our differences. There is no longer any common ground. If I have to debate with you that a couch is green rather than red, we will not be able to enter into an intelligent discussion if you don't even acknowledge that the couch exists. That is the state of affairs today.

Verses 21, 27-28 and 60-61 paint a startling picture regarding incurable diseases.

The Lord will plague you with diseases until He has destroyed you from the land you are entering to possess.

* * *

The Lord will afflict you with the boils of Egypt and with tumors, festering sores and the itch, from which you cannot be cured. The Lord will afflict you with madness, blindness and confusion of mind.

* * *

He will bring upon you all the diseases of Egypt that you dreaded, and they will cling to you. The Lord will also bring on you every kind of sickness and disaster not recorded in this Book of the Law, until you are destroyed.

In the context of Deuteronomy 28, verses 27-28 refer to the incurable diseases of Egypt. We know historically that the Egyptians were plagued with incurable sexually transmitted diseases. Today, we have several incurable STDs, not the least of which is AIDS. Today we not only have incurable diseases, we have new diseases which we have never encountered. We don't know their origin, let alone their cause or cure.

When I was pastoring, a doctor in my church who went to medical school in the 1960s stated that it was unheard of to think of a new disease. He was taught that we knew all the diseases. We just didn't know all the cures. Today, we are clueless as to the cures for many diseases. We have new diseases arising all the time. Existing diseases change forms. Creating antibodies has become a continuing challenge. We have new diseases unrelated to the previous ones we've encountered. We are on the verge of a viral epidemic in this country based upon our overuse of antibiotics. Incurable diseases are a natural consequence of rejecting God.

Verse 30 speaks of infidelity. It describes a situation where a man marries a woman but another man sleeps with her. Statistics that say divorce has leveled off or slightly decreased are inaccurate. These statistics are inaccurate because less people are getting married. More people are choosing to live with one another outside the confines of marriage. Sex is a big seller in the entertainment industry. Promiscuous sex is presented as the common way of life. President Clinton flaunted his sexual promiscuity. Instead of our religious leaders condemning him, one prominent leader suggested that President Clinton was simply a young, virile male succumbing to irresistible sexual instincts.

Another consequence of disobeying God is a weak military. Verse 36 indicates an army with very little central leadership. A foreign king will lead this army. Today, we are so wrapped up in a one world order concept under the leadership of the United Nations that we have forgotten our military dominance and our fierce independence.

A nation that rejects God will be a debtor nation. Verse 44 indicates that a nation rejecting God will be a debtor rather than a lender to its international neighbors. Today, we are the biggest debtor nation on earth. Our nation not only is in debt to other nations, our people are also burdened with debt. Quick financing with the allure of accumulating things has strapped our spendable income. Debt crushes America and breaks up families.

Deuteronomy 28, verses 56-57, illustrate the epitome of rejecting God:

> The most gentle and sensitive woman among you -- so sensitive and gentle that she would not venture to touch the ground with the sole of her foot -- will begrudge the husband she loves and her own son or daughter, the afterbirth from her womb and the children she bears. For she intends to eat them secretly during the siege and in the distress that your enemy will inflict on you and your cities.

Verse 56 pictures a delicate woman who is so tender that she can't even put her bare foot on the ground. This delicate picture of femininity will turn against her husband and hate him. She will also turn against her children and kill them. In context, the circumstance causing her to kill her children is famine. Then it was famine, today it's convenience. The woman who is supposed to be the protector of her child is now its destroyer. The womb is the most dangerous place for a child. Abortion has now moved to infanticide with partial birth abortion and sex selection. Euthanasia has already gripped part of the country with Oregon being the first state to officially legalize euthanasia.

The lessons of Deuteronomy 28 are clear. God has given us a choice. There are two paths we can follow. If we accept God and obey His commands, then the blessings of verses 1-14 are the inevitable result. However, if we reject God and do not follow His commandments, then verses 15-68 describe our ultimate demise. Deuteronomy clearly outlines the biblical basis for the proposition that God is the foundation for good government and national prosperity.

Historical Basis

Deuteronomy chapter 28 clearly outlines the proposition that God is the foundation of good government. Our early documents penned by our founding fathers also outline the historical basis for this same proposition. In 1776, the Declaration of Independence marked the beginning of our country's independence. Thomas Jefferson indicated that the Declaration of Independence was "an expression of the

American mind."[2] In relevant part, the Declaration states as follows:

> When in the course of human events, it becomes necessary for one people to dissolve the political bands which have connected them with another, and to assume among the Power of the earth, the separate and equal station to which the Laws of Nature and of Nature's God entitle them, a decent respect to the opinions of mankind requires that they should declare the causes which impel them to the separation.

> We hold these truths to be self-evident, that all men are created equal, that they are endowed by their Creator with certain unalienable Rights, that among these are Life, Liberty, and the pursuit of Happiness.

> That to secure these rights, Governments are instituted among Men, deriving their just powers from the consent of the governed.

> That whenever any Form of Government becomes destructive of these ends, it is the Right of the People to alter or to abolish it, to institute new Government, laying its foundation on such principles and organizing its powers in such form, as to them shall seem most likely to affect their

---

[2] Letter from Thomas Jefferson to Henry Lee, May 8, 1825, *reprinted in* William J. Bennett, ed., OUR SACRED HONOR 318.

Safety and Happiness . . . . But when a long train
of abuses and usurpations, pursuing invariably the
same Object, evinces a design to reduce them under
absolute Despotism, it is their right, it is their duty,
to throw off such Government, and to provide new
Guards for their future security . . . .

The first paragraph of the Declaration states that when
in the course of human history it becomes necessary for a
once unified people to dissolve their government, it is
necessary to document the reasons which impel them to the
separation. It was a bold step for our founding fathers to
separate from their homeland in order to create a separate
government with equal power and standing on earth as
Great Britain. The founders wanted to make clear the
reasons that caused this drastic step.

The second paragraph of the Declaration states the
central proposition: "We hold these truths to be self-
evident, . . ." These truths are not debatable. They are
self-evident. These truths predate government. No form of
government can add to or take away from these truths.
These truths cannot be modified. These truths are not up
for vote or debate. They are self-evident and God-given.
What are these truths?

These self-evident truths are that all men are created
equal, they are endowed with certain unalienable rights, that
among these are life, liberty, and the pursuit of happiness.
The rights delineated are unalienable. Government cannot
take them away and government cannot give them. The
Supreme Court has no jurisdiction to vote on these rights.

In other words, the Supreme Court and the other branches of government must protect these rights.

The Declaration answers the question about what is government and why do we need government. Whenever we come together to form a social relationship, we create rules to govern our interaction. It doesn't matter what title we give these rules. The rules we make we call "government." Whether it is a republic, a democracy, an oligarchy, a monarchy, or communism, it is still called "government." We assign tasks to one another and we outline our various rights. The Declaration clearly indicates that in order "to secure these rights, governments are instituted among men, deriving their just powers from the consent of the governed."

The sole purpose of government is to secure "these rights", namely the rights to equality, to life, liberty, and the pursuit of happiness. That is the purpose of government. When viewed properly, the historical basis for government is to secure certain God-given, unalienable rights. The role of government is therefore limited. Government is to be a protector of God-given rights, not an enemy.

However, "whenever any form of government becomes destructive of these ends, it is the right of the people to alter or to abolish it, . . ." It is therefore the right of the people "to institute new government, laying its foundation on such principles and organizing its powers in such form, as to them shall seem most likely to affect their Safety and Happiness." However, when government evinces a pattern of abuses which inevitably pursue the same object to reduce the governed under absolute despotism, then "it is their right, it is their duty, to throw off such government, and to provide new guards for their future security . . . ." The Declaration is clear that rebellion against government should not occur for a simple mistake or an occasional misstep. However, when government, whatever its form, sets a course to no longer protect these God-given, unalienable rights, it is not only our right, but it is our "duty" to alter, or if necessary, to abolish it. This is the point in history at which our early leaders found themselves. The American Revolution must not be considered a one-time forgotten event. Revolution may be necessary at any given point in history whenever government no longer protects our God-given, unalienable rights.

The purpose of government is to preserve life, liberty, and the pursuit of happiness. There is no question that our early founders presupposed our country was to be based upon Jesus Christ and Judeo-Christian principles of morality and virtue.

The first Colonial grant from Queen Elizabeth to Sir Walter Raleigh in 1584 was stipulated for the purpose to enact laws provided "they be not against the true Christian faith."[3] In other words, the monetary grant used to form this new colony had a stipulation. No law should be enacted under this grant that would in any way be contrary to the true Christian faith.

---

[3] *The Church of the Holy Trinity v. United States*, 143 U.S. 457, 466 (1892).

The United States Supreme Court in 1872 in the case of *The Church of the Holy Trinity* stated on three separate occasions that "this is a Christian nation", "we are a Christian people" and "this is a Christian nation."[4]

George Washington, our first general and first President of the United States, stated, "Reason and experience both forbid us to expect that national morality can prevail in the exclusion of religious principle."[5]

John Quincy Adams, the sixth United States President, stated that the "highest glory of the American Revolution was this: it connected in one indissoluble bond, the principles of civil government with the principles of Christianity."[6] Can you imagine if today's politicians would echo the words of John Quincy Adams? The liberal media would crucify them.

John Adams, our first Vice President and second President, hit the nail on the head when he stated:

> We have no government armed with power capable of contending with human passions unbridled by morality and religion. Avarice, ambition, revenge, or gallantry, would break the strongest cords of our Constitution as a whale goes through a net. *Our*

---

[4] *Id.* at 471.

[5] Washington, Farewell Address, September 17, 1796, *reprinted in* Johnson, GEORGE WASHINGTON THE CHRISTIAN 217-18.

[6] J. Wingate Thornton, THE PULPIT OF THE AMERICAN REVOLUTION (1860) (*reprinted by* Burt Franklin, NY 1970) XXIX.

Constitution was made only for a moral and religious people. It is wholly inadequate to the government of any other.[7]

The founders presupposed that we, the governed, would have self-restraint. Unbridled human passion results in destruction and chaos. Our passions must be restrained. These passions will be restrained either internally or externally. The founders presupposed that our passions would be self-restrained. We have an internal restraint based upon Jesus Christ and Judeo-Christian morality and virtue. In the absence of this self-restraint, the only other alternative is external restraint. If we are not self-restrained, then the government must restrain us.

Our constitutional republic was designed as a limited form of government with very little external restraints on the people. Few restraints were necessary because the founders presupposed self-restraint. If we are not self-restrained, then the liberties acknowledged and protected by our Constitution will result in chaos. That is why it is so easy in this country for a terrorist to cause destruction.

For example, if parents don't restrain their children from being downtown after midnight during the week, then government will by enacting curfew laws. Government will take away our external liberties to the extent that our

---

[7] John Adams, Letter "To the Officers of the First Brigade of the Third Division of the Militia of Massachusetts," October 11, 1798, *reprinted in* Bennett, OUR SACRED HONOR 370 (emphasis added).

internal liberty is unrestrained. No form of government, republic or dictatorship, can restrain an unrestrained people.

On July 21, 1789, the First Continental Congress adopted the Northwest Ordinance that was originally drafted by Thomas Jefferson and enacted by Congress under the Articles of Confederation on July 13, 1787. The Ordinance states: "Religion, morality and knowledge, being necessary to good government and the happiness of mankind, schools and the means of education shall be forever encouraged."[8] Since religion and morality were necessary to good government, the means of inculcating these values were through public schools. There was no thought of "separation of church and state" between religion and the public schools at the time of the First Continental Congress. Indeed, public schools were considered the vehicle through which religion and morality would be taught to our new generation.

Dr. Benjamin Rush, one of the signers of the Declaration, stated the following in *A Defense of the Use of the Bible in Schools*:

The only means of establishing and perpetrating our republican forms of government . . . is the

---

[8] Ord. of 1789, July 13, 1789, Art. A III, *reprinted in* DOCUMENTS ILLUSTRATIVE OF THE FORMATION OF THE UNION OF AMERICAN STATES 52 (1927).

universal education of our youth in the principles of Christianity by the means of the Bible.[9]

The first compulsory school law was entitled, "The Old Deluder Satan Act." Drafted in 1647, the law stated that because "one chief project of that old deluder, Satan, [is] to keep men from the knowledge of the Scriptures," public schools were necessary to teach people to read.[10]

Harvard was the first college in America. Founded in 1636, the official Harvard motto was, "For Christ and the Church."[11] Harvard, Princeton, Yale, William and Mary, Rutgers and Columbia are just a few of the well known universities that had Christian origins. Of the one hundred twenty-six original colleges in America, one hundred twenty-three were based on Christian principles.[12]

Benjamin Harris's school textbook, *The New England Primer*, was one of the most influential school textbooks in the history of American education. It was first printed in 1690 and was continually used from then until 1900, a span of two hundred and ten years. In a 1777 edition, the first

---

[9] Benjamin Rush, ESSAYS, LITERARY, MORAL, AND PHILOSOPHICAL 93-94 (1806).

[10] David Barton, EDUCATION AND THE FOUNDING FATHERS 4.

[11] William J. Federer, AMERICA'S GOD AND COUNTRY ENCYCLOPEDIA OF QUOTATIONS 282.

[12] Barton, EDUCATION AND THE FOUNDING FATHERS 7.

section contained the rhyming alphabet. A partial example includes the following:

A. In Adam's fall we sinned all.
C. Christ crucify'd for sinners dy'd.
D. The deluge drown'd the Earth around.

* * *

H. My book and heart must never part.

* * *

Z. Zaccheus did climb the tree our Lord to see.

In another section, *The New England Primer* contained the alphabet with Bible verses:

E. Except a man be born again he cannot see the kingdom of God.

* * *

L. Liars shall have their part in the lake which burns with fire and brimstone.

* * *

N. Now is the accepted time, now is the day of Salvation.

Since there were no grade levels at the time of our founding fathers, the following test would be equivalent to the first grade. See how well you score.

What offices does Christ execute as our Redeemer?
How does Christ execute the office of a prophet?

How does Christ execute the office of a priest?
How does Christ execute the office of a king?
Which is the fifth commandment?
What is required in the fifth commandment?
What is forbidden in the fifth commandment?
What is the reason annexed in the fifth commandment?
Bonus question -- What are the benefits which in this life do accompany or flow from justification, adoption and sanctification?

Remember the above test was universally distributed in all schools. Today, how would our public school students score on this test? Would our Sunday School students pass this test? Though I won't ask you, ask yourself how well you scored.[13]

Noah Webster graduated from Yale University. He was an expert in grammar and mastered twenty-eight languages. Though he authored many school textbooks, his most famous one was produced in 1828, known as the *American Dictionary of the English Language*. In less than two decades, approximately twenty-four million copies of his dictionaries had been sold. Noah Webster was clearly a Christian as evidenced by his personal testimony contained in the 1854 edition of the dictionary. Noah Webster believed that Christianity was central to education and government:

---

[13]In order to underscore the dumbing down of America, see Appendix C. Contained therein is a final exam from 1895 given to eighth grade students in Salina, Kansas

The Christian religion is the most important and one of the first things in which all children under a free government, ought to be instructed . . . No truth is more evident to my mind than that the Christian religion must be the basis of any government intended to secure the rights and privileges of a free people.[14]

If anyone doubts the effectiveness of this country's early education, try spelling the following words: loquacious, sagacious, mucilaginous, legerdemain, duodecimo, imperceptibility, perpendicularity, and incomprehensibility. These words were required spelling for what we would classify today as elementary students.

Clearly there is a biblical and historical base for the proposition that God is the foundation of good government and national prosperity. This proposition is presupposed in Deuteronomy chapter 28. It is also presupposed in America's founding documents. The Declaration of Independence is probably the best historical document that outlines the purpose and place of government and religion. Government's role is to protect and preserve certain God-given, unalienable, self-evident rights. Government will self destruct if the governed are no longer self-restrained by Judeo-Christian morality and virtue. Government must be changed, or if necessary abolished, if it no longer protects these liberties.

---

[14] Barton, EDUCATION AND THE FOUNDING FATHERS 14-15.

2

Our Country Has Displaced God As Our Foundation

Today our country has displaced God as our foundation and replaced Him with human reason. The result is uncontrolled human passion which will inevitably lead to self-destruction.

Separation of Church and State

This country was established upon the assumption that religion was essential to good government. On July 13, 1787, the Continental Congress enacted the Northwest Ordinance, which stated: "Religion, morality and knowledge, being necessary to good government and the happiness of mankind, schools and the means of education shall be forever encouraged."[1] The First Amendment prohibited the federal government from establishing a religion to which the several states must pay homage. The First Amendment provided assurance that the federal government would not meddle in the affairs of religion within the sovereign states.

Today, groups like the American Civil Liberties Union and Americans United for Separation of Church and State have attempted to create an environment wherein

---

[1]Ord. of 1789, July 13, 1789, Art. A III, *reprinted in* DOCUMENTS ILLUSTRATIVE OF THE FORMATION OF THE UNION OF AMERICAN STATES 52 (1927).

government and religion are adversaries. Their favorite phrase has been "separation of church and state." These groups have intoned the mantra of "separation of church and state" so long that many people believe the phrase is in the Constitution. In Proverbs Chapter 18, verse 16, the Bible says, "He who states his case first seems right until another comes to challenge him." I'm sure you have seen legal arguments on television where the prosecution argues to the jury that the defendant is guilty. Once the prosecution finishes the opening presentation, you believe that the defendant is guilty. However, after the defense attorney completes the rebuttal presentation of the argument, you may be confused, or at least you acknowledge that the case is not clear cut.

The same is true with the phrase "separation of church and state." The ACLU and the liberal media have touted the phrase so many times that most people believe the phrase is in the Constitution. Nowhere is "separation of church and state" referenced in the Constitution. This phrase was in the former Soviet Union's Constitution, but it has never been part of the United States Constitution.

Justice Oliver Wendell Holmes once said, "It is one of the misfortunes of the law that ideas become encysted in phrases, and thereafter for a long time cease to provoke further analysis."[2] The phrase, "separation of church and state," has become one of these misfortunes of law.

---

[2] *Hyde v. United States*, 225 U.S. 347, 384 (1912) (Holmes, J., dissenting).

In 1947 the Supreme Court popularized Thomas Jefferson's phrase "wall of separation between church and state."[3] Taking the Jefferson metaphor out of context, strict separationists have often used the phrase to silence Christians and to limit any Christian influence from affecting the political system. To understand Jefferson's "wall of separation," we should return to the original context in which it was written. Jefferson himself once wrote:

> On every question of construction, [we must] carry ourselves back to the time when the constitution was adopted, recollect the spirit manifested in the debates, and instead of trying what meaning may be squeezed out of the text, or invented against it, conform to the probable one in which it was a part.[4]

Thomas Jefferson was inaugurated as the third President on March 4, 1801. On October 7, 1801, a committee of the Danbury Baptist Association wrote a congratulatory letter to Jefferson on his election as President. Organized in 1790, the Danbury Baptist Association was an alliance of churches in Western Connecticut. The Baptists were a religious

---

[3] *See Everson v. Bd. of Educ.*, 330 U.S. 1 (1947). *See also McCollum v. Bd. of Educ.*, 333 U.S. 203, 211 (1948).

[4] Thomas Jefferson to Messrs. Nehemiah Dodge, Ephraim Robbins and Stephen S. Nelson, a Committee of the Danbury Baptist Association in the State of Connecticut, January 1, 1802, Presidential Papers Microfilm, THOMAS JEFFERSON PAPERS, Manuscript Division, Library of Congress, Ser. I, reel 25, November. 15, 1801 – March 31, 1802; Jefferson to William Johnson, June 12, 1823, Presidential Papers Microfilm, THOMAS JEFFERSON PAPERS, Manuscript Division, Library of Congress, Ser. I, reel 70. The letters referenced herein can be found at the above citation.

minority in the state of Connecticut where
Congregationalism was the established church.[5]

The concern of the Danbury Baptist Association is
understandable once we consider the background of church-
state relations in Great Britain. The Association eschewed
the kind of state sponsored enforcement of religion that had
been the norm in Great Britain.

The Danbury Baptist Association committee wrote to
the President stating, "Religion is at all times and places a
Matter between God and Individuals -- that no man ought to
suffer in Name, person or affects on account of his religious
Opinions."[6] The Danbury Baptists believed that religion was
an unalienable right and they hoped that Jefferson would
raise the consciousness of the people to recognize religious
freedom as unalienable. However, the Danbury Baptists
acknowledged that the President of the United States was
not a "national Legislator" and they also understood that the
"national government cannot destroy the Laws of each
State."[7] In other words, they recognized Jefferson's limited
influence as the federal executive on the individual states.

Jefferson did not necessarily like receiving mail as
President, but he generally endeavored to turn his responses
into an opportunity to sow what he called "useful truths"

---

[5] Daniel Dreisbach, "Sowing Useful Truths and Principles": The
Danbury Baptists, Thomas Jefferson, and the "Wall of Separation," 39
JOURNAL OF CHURCH AND STATE 455, 459 (1997).

[6] Id. at 460.

[7] Id.

and principles among the people so that the ideas might take political root. He therefore took this opportunity to explain why he as President, contrary to his predecessors, did not proclaim national days of fasting and prayer.

Jefferson's letter went through at least two drafts. Part of the first draft reads as follows:

> Believing with you that religion is a matter which lies solely between man & his god, that he owes account to none other for his faith or his worship, that legitimate powers of government reach actions only and not opinions, I contemplate with sovereign reverence that act of the whole American people which declared that their legislature should make no law respecting an establishment of religion, or prohibiting the free exercise thereof; thus building a wall of separation between church and state. Congress thus inhibited from acts respecting religion, and the Executive authorized only to execute their acts, I have refrained from prescribing even occasional performances of devotion...[8]

Jefferson asked Levi Lincoln, the Attorney General, and Gideon Granger, the Postmaster General, to comment on his draft. In a letter to Mr. Lincoln, Jefferson stated he wanted to take the occasion to explain why he did not "proclaim national fastings & thanksgivings, as my predecessors did."[9] He knew that the response would "give great offense to the

---

[8] *Id.* at 462.

[9] *Id.* at 463 n. 16.

New England clergy" and he advised Lincoln that he should suggest necessary changes.[10]

Mr. Lincoln responded that the five New England states have always been in the habit of "observing fasts and thanksgivings in performance of proclamations from the respective Executives" and that this "custom is venerable being handed down from our ancestors."[11] Lincoln therefore struck through the last sentence of the above quoted letter about Jefferson refraining from prescribing even occasional performances of devotion. Jefferson penned a note in the margin that this paragraph was omitted because "it might give uneasiness to some of our republican friends in the eastern states where the proclamation of thanksgivings" by their state executives is respected.[12]

To understand Jefferson's use of the wall metaphor in his letter to the Danbury Baptist Association, we must compare his other writings. On March 4, 1805, in Jefferson's Second Inaugural Address, he stated as follows:

> In matters of religion, I have considered that its free exercise is placed by the Constitution independent of the powers of the General [i.e., federal] Government. I have therefore undertaken, on no occasion, to prescribe the religious exercises suited to it; but have left them, as the Constitution found them, under the direction and discipline of State or

---

[10] *Id.* at 465.

[11] *Id.* at 466.

[12] *Id.* at 462 n. 13.

Church authorities acknowledged by the several religious societies.[13]

Then on January 23, 1808, Jefferson wrote in response to a letter received by Reverend Samuel Miller, who requested him to declare a national day of thanksgiving and prayer:

> I consider the government of the United States as interdicted by the Constitution from intermeddling with religious institutions, their doctrines, discipline, or exercises. This results not only from the provisions that no law shall be made respecting the establishment or free exercise of religion [First Amendment], but from that also which reserves to the States the powers not delegated to the United States [Tenth Amendment]. Certainly no power to prescribe any religious exercise, or to assume authority in religious discipline, has been delegated to the General [i.e., federal] Government. It must then rest with the States, as far as it can be in any human authority.[14]

* * *

I am aware that the practice of my predecessors may be quoted. But I have every belief, that the

---

[13] Thomas Jefferson to the Reverend Samuel Miller, January 23, 1808, in Andrew A. Lipscomb *et al.*, eds., THE WRITINGS OF THOMAS JEFFERSON 11:428; Jefferson, Second Inaugural Address, March 4, 1805, in Andrew A. Lipscomb *et al.*, eds., THE WRITINGS OF THOMAS JEFFERSON 3:378.

[14] Thomas Jefferson to the Reverend Samuel Miller, January 23, 1808, in THE WRITINGS OF THOMAS JEFFERSON 11:428.

example of State executives led to the assumption of
that authority by the General Government, without
due examination, which would have discovered that
what might be a right in State government, was a
violation of that right when assumed by another....
[C]ivil powers alone have been given to the
President of the United States, and no authority to
direct the religious exercises of his constituents.[15]

Comparing these two responses to his actions in the
state government of Virginia show the true intent of
Jefferson's wall metaphor. As a member of the House of
Burgesses, on May 24, 1774, Jefferson participated in
drafting and enacting a resolution designating a "Day of
Fasting, Humiliation, and Prayer."[16] This resolution
occurred only a few days before he wrote "A Bill for
Establishing Religious Freedom." In 1779, while Jefferson
was governor of Virginia, he issued a proclamation
decreeing a day "of publick and solemn thanksgiving and
prayer to Almighty God." In the late 1770's, as chair of the
Virginia committee of Revisers, Jefferson was the chief
architect of a measure entitled, "A Bill for Appointing Days
of Public Fasting and Thanksgiving." Interestingly, this bill
authorized the governor, or Chief Magistrate with the
advice of Counsel, to designate days of thanksgiving and
fasting and, required that the public be notified by
proclamation. The bill also provided that "[e]very minister
of the gospel shall on each day so to be appointed, attend
and perform divine service and preach a sermon, or

---

[15] *Id.* at 11:430.

[16] J. Body, ed., THE PAPERS OF JEFFERSON 1:105.

discourse, suited to the occasion, in his church, on pain of forfeiting fifty pounds for every failure, not having a reasonable excuse."[17] Though the bill was never enacted, Jefferson was its chief architect, and the sponsor was none other than James Madison.

So what did Jefferson mean when he used the "wall" metaphor? Jefferson undoubtedly meant that the First Amendment prohibited the federal Congress from enacting any law respecting an establishment of religion or prohibiting the free exercise thereof. As the chief executive of the federal government, the President's duty was to carry out the directives of Congress. If Congress had no authority in matters of religion, then neither did the President. Religion was clearly within the jurisdiction of the church and states. As a state legislator, Jefferson saw no problem with proclaiming days of thanksgiving and prayer, and even on one occasion prescribed a penalty to the clergy for failure to abide by these state proclamations. Jefferson believed that the Constitution created a limited government and that the states retained the authority over matters of religion not only through the First Amendment but also through the Tenth Amendment.[18] The federal government

---

[17] *Report of the Committee of Revisors Appointed by the General Assembly of Virginia in MDCCLXXVI* (Richmond, Va., 1984) 59-60; Julian P. Boyd, *et al.*, eds., THE PAPERS OF THOMAS JEFFERSON 2:556.

[18] In the Kentucky-Virginia Resolutions of 1798, Jefferson wrote that the powers not delegated to the United States are reserved to the States and that "no power over the freedom of religion, freedom of speech, or freedom of the press being delegated to the United States by the Constitution, nor prohibited by it to the States, all lawful powers respecting the same did of right remain, and were reserved to the States, or to the people. . . [and are] withheld from the cognizance of

had absolutely no jurisdiction over religion, as that matter was left where the Constitution found it, namely with the individual churches and the several states.

In summary, the First Amendment says more about federalism than religious freedom. In other words, the purpose of the First Amendment was to declare that the federal government had absolutely no jurisdiction in matters of religion. It could neither establish a religion, nor prohibit the free exercise of religion. The First Amendment clearly erected a barrier between the federal government and religion on a state level. If a state chose to have no religion, or to have an established religion, the federal government had no jurisdiction one way or the other. This is what Thomas Jefferson meant by the "wall of separation." In context, the word "state" really referred to the federal government. The First Amendment did not apply to the states. It was only applicable as a restraint against the federal government. The problem arose in 1940[19] and then again in 1947[20] when the Supreme Court applied the First Amendment to the states. This turned the First Amendment on its head, and completely inverted its meaning.[21] The First Amendment was never meant to be a restraint on state

---

federal tribunals." THE KENTUCKY-VIRGINIA RESOLUTIONS AND MR. MADISON'S REPORT OF 1799 2-3.

[19] *See Cantwell v. Connecticut*, 310 U.S. 296 (1940).

[20] *See Everson*, 330 U.S. at 1.

[21] One of the early Supreme Court Justices, Joseph Story, wrote that "the whole power over the subject of religion is left exclusively to the state governments, to be acted upon according to their own sense of justice, and the state constitutions. . ." J. Story, COMMENTARIES ON THE CONSTITUTION § 1879 (1833).

government. It was only applicable to the federal government. When the Supreme Court turned the First Amendment around 180 degrees and used Jefferson's comment in the process, it not only perverted the First Amendment, but misconstrued the intent of Jefferson's letter.

There is nothing wrong with the way Jefferson used the "wall of separation between church and state" metaphor. The problem has arisen when the Supreme Court in 1947 erroneously picked up the metaphor and attempted to construct a constitutional principal. While the metaphor understood in its proper context is useful, we might do well to heed the words of the United States Supreme Court Justice William Rehnquist:

> The "wall of separation between church and State" is a metaphor based on bad history, a metaphor which has proved useless as a guide to judging. It should be frankly and explicitly abandoned.[22]

Jefferson used the phrase "wall of separation between church and state" as a means of expressing his republican view that the federal or general government should not interfere with religious matters among the several states. In its proper context, the phrase represents a clear expression of state autonomy.

Accordingly, Jefferson saw no contradiction in authoring a religious proclamation to be used by

---

[22] *Wallace v. Jaffree*, 472 U.S. 38, 106 (Rehnquist, J., dissenting).

state officials and refusing to issue similar religious proclamations as president of the United States. His wall had less to do with the separation of church and *all* civil government than with the separation of federal and state governments.[23]

The "wall of separation between church and state" phrase as understood by Jefferson was never meant to exclude people of faith from influencing and shaping government. Jefferson would be shocked to learn that his letter has been used as a weapon against religion. He would never countenance such shabby and distorted use of history.

The Supreme Court as Change Agent

The biggest destroyer of American values and religious freedom in this country has been the United States Supreme Court. Though originally the Supreme Court had no jurisdiction over religious matters among the individual states, it nevertheless usurped this authority and this power grab went unchallenged by the governed. We have allowed the Supreme Court to amass power that it was never granted. With its new self-appointed power unchecked by the people, the Supreme Court turned its destructive cannons on religion and public schools in 1962 and 1963. During those years, the Supreme Court ruled school-sponsored prayer and Bible reading unconstitutional. In one case, the Supreme Court quoted an alleged expert's testimony in the trial court where he stated: "If portions of the New Testament were read without explanation, they

---

[23] Daniel Dreisbach, *Thomas Jefferson and the Danbury Baptists Revisited*, 56:4 WILLIAM AND MARY QUARTERLY 805, 812 (1999).

could be and ... had been psychologically harmful to the child..."[24]

In 1980 the Supreme Court realigned its war cannons toward the public schools one more time. This time, the Court stripped the Ten Commandments from a classroom bulletin board in a Kentucky public school. The rationale used by the Supreme Court was that the students might actually view the Ten Commandments as they hung on the classroom bulletin board and be induced to observe their dictates. If this occurred, the Court felt the result would be an unconstitutional establishment of religion.[25]   The Supreme Court had the audacity to state the following:

If the posted copies of the Ten Commandments are to have any effect at all, it will be to induce the schoolchildren to read, meditate upon, perhaps to venerate and obey, the Commandments. However desirable this might be as a matter of private devotion, it is not a permissible state objective under the Establishment Clause.[26]

The Supreme Court was at least right about one thing. Since the Court removed the Ten Commandments, students no longer observe them. Metal detectors have now replaced the Ten Commandments.

---

[24] *School Dist. of Abington Township v. Schempp*, 374 U.S. 203, 209 (1963).

[25] *Stone v. Graham*, 449 U.S. 39 (1980).

[26] *Id.* at 42.

The "separation of church and state" mantra intoned by the ACLU has wrought untold damage to America. The following cases are illustrations of situations that we have encountered at Liberty Counsel. Though some of these cases may seem bizarre, we have investigated each one and found the facts to be true.

In Duluth, Minnesota, an accountant became blind from diabetes. He required dialysis three times per week. He received this dialysis at a local hospital. While there, he watched religious programming on his private T.V. He also occasionally shared his faith in Christ with other willing patients. The head nurse told him that he could no longer watch religious programming on his own T.V. and he must stop talking about Jesus to other patients. If he did not cease this activity, she threatened to unplug him from the dialysis machine and refuse him further treatment. The facts are so shocking that we thought this man must be disruptive. We interviewed his driver who confirmed the facts. We also spoke to other patients. No other patient had ever complained. The only one who had complained was the head nurse. Her threats to unplug him and refuse treatment were literally death threats engendered solely by his Christian witness.

In West Allis, Wisconsin, Chris Pfeifer founded the Genesis Commission. Chris has not always been a Christian. In fact, at one time he was an agnostic steeped in evolution. After he accepted Christ, he began studying the origins of the universe. He then became convinced of creation.

Chris applied to use a public meeting room in a public library in West Allis. The name of the room was the Constitution Room. The Policy provided that anyone could use the room for meetings, but the Policy prohibited any religious viewpoint. When Chris handed in his application, he was told that it would probably be denied because of the Christian nature of his meeting. He was also told that he could not have prayer in the Constitution Room. Once the application was denied, Liberty Counsel filed suit. During the depositions, the Library Director acknowledged that any topic can be discussed in the Constitution Room except religion. In fact, at the conclusion of the deposition, I placed various library books on the desk in front of the Director. He acknowledged that these books were from the Library. These books addressed Christianity and creation. He stated that Chris could read these books privately by himself in a library carrel, but he could not walk across the hall to the Constitution Room and tell others about them because that would be religious instruction prohibited by the Policy.[27]

In Crown Point, Indiana, the Northwest Community Church and its pastor, Steve Buchelt, sought to rent school facilities for his young new church. His church began meeting at the school auditorium on Sunday mornings. However, when the rental contract was presented to the Superintendent for final approval, the Superintendent evicted the church without notice. The Policy allowed secular groups to rent the school facilities but not religious groups.

---

[27] *Pfeifer v. City of West Allis*, 91 F. Supp.2d 1253 (E.D. Wis. 2000).

After Liberty Counsel filed suit, the School Board Attorney was terminated and we were able to resolve the case by drafting a new Policy. Several weeks after the church began meeting in the school auditorium I had the pleasure of preaching at the church. I was surprised to observe a plaque in the auditorium foyer that read, "Freedom Shrine", surrounded by historical documents. One of the documents was The Northwest Ordinance. I pointed out a sentence in the Ordinance to Pastor Buchelt that read, "Religion, morality and education, being necessary to good government and the happiness of mankind, schools and the means of education shall be forever encouraged." Had the school officials and their attorney read and understood these documents, which have been displayed in the auditorium for years, they would have welcomed the church.

In Deland, Florida, a third grade teacher told her students they could select any book to bring to class and read as long as the book did not mention God. In Itheca, New York, a student was told by her teacher to remove her book cover because it listed the Ten Commandments. The teacher stated that the book cover could not be brought into the public schools because of the "separation of church and state." The teacher also told the student that she could no longer wear her gold cross necklace on the outside of her blouse. She was told to tuck the cross under her blouse.

In Orlando, Florida, a six-year-old was asked by his fellow classmate at recess about the meaning of Easter. He told his classmate that it was about God raising Jesus from the dead. When the teacher overheard him, she told him that he could not talk about God in the public schools because of the "separation of church and state."

Jessie was an eleven-year-old special needs child. Jessie's class threw a birthday party for her. Jessie got excited so her mother, who attended the party, took Jessie into the kitchen to pray with her. A teacher's aide and another student overheard Jessie's mother praying and told school officials. The school officials then told Jessie's mother that she could never again pray with her daughter while she was on the school campus.

When Christopher was in the second grade, his teacher asked the class to make a Valentine card as a school project. His card said, "Roses are red. Violets are blue. Did you know that Jesus loves you?" When he handed in his card like the other students, the teacher singled out his card and gave it back. She said that he could not use the word "Jesus" in public school because it violates the "separation of church and state."

In the case of *Adler v. Duval County School Board*,[28] the school has a policy that provides students with an opportunity to present a two minute message at the beginning and/or conclusion of their graduation. The Policy never mentions the word "prayer." The students can have any message, whether it's secular, sacred, profane or profound. The ACLU filed suit claiming that the students might use the two minute message for some kind of religious topic or worse - they might even pray. The ACLU argued that if the students said anything religious, this

---

[28]206 F.3d 1070 (11th Cir. 2000) (en banc).

would somehow violate the Constitution. Fortunately we have successfully defended against the ACLU. However, this case illustrates the absurdity of the ACLU's "separation of church and state" position. In the view of the ACLU, students can say anything they want as long as it is not religious. This position is a far cry from the understanding of our founding fathers.

In Waukesha, Wisconsin, Robert Thompson desired to pass out Bibles and pocket-sized copies of the United States Constitution and the Declaration of Independence in a public park. He was surprised to come across the county park ordinance that stated if anyone wanted to talk about politics or religion with another person in the park, they first needed to receive prior permission from county officials. Also, the policy completely prohibited the distribution of any religious or political material in the public park. Robert thought surely this must be a mistake, so he went to the county office and was told by officials that he could not pass out religious or political literature and if he didn't like the Ordinance, he could sue them. We did, and we won. The policy has now been redrafted and Robert can pass out his Bibles.

In Marietta, Georgia, Art and Norma Ellison host a Friday evening prayer meeting in their home as part of cell group meetings of their local church. Approximately six to eight people attend the Friday evening meetings. Most of the time, everyone parks in the Ellison's driveway. There is no loud music and no disruption. To their astonishment, Art and Norma received a letter from the Planning and Zoning Commission stating that the couple was in violation of a zoning code because their house was in a residential district and they were conducting "church" in an unauthorized area. The letter warned that the couple must immediately cease and desist the home prayer meeting. We found out that the City allowed other secular meetings such as Boy Scouts, Girl Scouts, Amway and Mary Kay meetings in local homes. Other people gathered to watch Monday night football. On the eve of filing a lawsuit, I faxed a letter to the City zoning officials demanding that the City retract the letter immediately or otherwise face a federal suit. Fortunately, the City retracted the letter. However, in another case, a couple in Denver, Colorado, had to litigate the issue because there the City zoning officials stated that the prayer meeting could be conducted in a home one time per month, but anything more than that violates the City zoning laws.

In Syracuse, New York, Antonio Peck attended kindergarten. The teacher told the class to draw a poster reflecting their understanding of the environment. Antonio's first poster had various religious drawings with a message at the top which stated, "The only way to save the world." The obvious implication from Antonio's viewpoint is that God is the only way to save the environment. The teacher rejected the poster because it was religious. Antonio was confused and hurt. He drew a second poster. This poster contained a crayon drawing of stick people depositing trash in a garbage can, others putting trash in a recycle bin, the world with cutout children holding hands and circling the globe, and a picture on the left side of the poster of a robed man kneeling down on one knee with both hands stretched forth to the sky. Antonio clearly understood this person to be Jesus. When he handed in this poster, it was displayed in the cafeteria with the posters of the other four kindergarten classes of approximately eighty students. However, Antonio's poster, unlike the other students, was folded in half so that the picture of Jesus could not be seen. The school teacher took the position that she could not display the poster because it was religious. The Principal and the Superintendent refused to budge and Liberty Counsel was forced to file a federal lawsuit.

In Homestead, Florida, Reverend Kenneth Greathouse sought to establish a new church called Apostolic Worship Center. He was temporarily renting space in a storefront business district. He was told he had to leave the facilities or otherwise face fines because the code was being redrafted. The City redrafted its zoning code so that churches coming into the business district can only reside there for a maximum of two years. After that, the churches needed to move and the location could never again be used by any religious institution. When the City refused to repeal this unconstitutional ordinance, Liberty Counsel filed suit.

College students who attend the Miami-Dade Community College set aside one week toward the end of the summer to pass out a business-sized card containing the following message: "The call you'll never forget." Underneath the message was a local telephone number. This number dialed their local church where the caller would receive a voice recorded message of the gospel. The students wanted to hand out these cards to other students on campus during nonclass time. To their surprise they were confronted by college security officers and were told that they could not hand out the cards on campus. The students could not believe this was happening. The students returned on the following day to pass out the cards and again were confronted by security officers. This time the officers phoned a police officer who threatened arrest if they continued to hand out the cards. Liberty Counsel filed suit on behalf of the students.

In Missouri and Louisiana, public school students were told they could not pass out the Truth For Youth Bible to fellow classmates during the annual See You At The Pole event. Fortunately Liberty Counsel was able to intervene in both of these matters to resolve them. One was resolved on the eve of the event short of litigation but the other required a federal lawsuit.

When Joshua Burton was in the fourth grade, he brought his Bible to school to read on a bench by himself before the beginning of the school day. The teacher told him he could not bring his Bible to school because of the "separation of church and state." When Joshua told his father, his father thought this must be a misunderstanding and surely Joshua could bring his Bible to school. On another day, Joshua did bring his Bible to school, and even though he had the Bible closed and did not read it, the teacher approached him and in front of the class, took his Bible, and then escorted Joshua to the cafeteria where he had to stay in detention all day, solely for bringing his Bible to school.

I could list hundreds and hundreds of examples of religious discrimination that we have handled at Liberty Counsel. Some of these situations are so bizarre you would think they are a creation of someone's distorted imagination.

We have been surprised to determine after investigation that rampant discrimination is taking place all across America. Part of the discrimination is based upon an ignorance of the Constitution. The mantra of "separation of church and state" has been repeated so many times that most people understand it to mean that religious faith and practice must be cleansed from the public. Some believe that the only place for religion is within the four walls of the church or possibly in the closet. Fortunately most of these situations resolve through education. However, the cases that we encounter are simply the tip of the iceberg. Those instances which do not resolve through education oftentimes require litigation. Our liberties hang in a delicate balance and we must be vigilant to protect them at all cost.

As a result of this constitutional schizophrenia sucking religion from our public schools, America has developed quite a track record. This track record is not only graced with a dumbing down of our students, it is now laced with a trail of blood. The following illustrates a startling trend in our public school system.

• October 1, 1997 -- in Pearl, Mississippi, a sixteen-year-old boy killed his mother and shot nine students, killing two.

• December 1, 1997 -- in Paducah, Kentucky, while students were leaving a Bible Club prayer meeting on school campus, a fourteen-year-old boy shot and killed three fellow students and wounded five others.

• March 24, 1998 -- in Jonesboro, Arkansas, two boys, ages eleven and thirteen, opened fire killing four girls and a teacher, wounding ten others.

• April 24, 1998 -- in Edinboro, Pennsylvania, a fourteen-year-old student shot to death a science teacher in front of other students at an eighth grade dance.

• May 19, 1998 -- in Fayetteville, Tennessee, an eighteen-year-old honor student opened fire in a high school parking lot, killing a classmate who was dating his ex-girlfriend.

• April 16, 1999 -- in Notus, Idaho, a tenth grade student opened fire in a school hallway. Fortunately no one was injured.

• April 20, 1999 -- in Littleton, Colorado, two boys, ages seventeen and eighteen, shot and killed twelve classmates and one teacher, wounding twenty-three others before killing themselves. Many of these shootings were religiously motivated. The gunmen asked some of the students whether they believed in Jesus. When the students said yes, the gunmen murdered them.

• April 22, 1999 -- in Scotlandville, Louisiana, a fourteen-year-old fired a weapon from a parking lot aiming for a student he had previously argued with, but instead he injured a fourteen-year-old girl standing nearby.

• April 29, 1999 -- in Brooklyn, New York, five middle school students were taken into custody on charges of conspiracy to commit murder, arson and manufacturing explosives. They intended to blow up their school.

- May 20, 1999 -- in Conyers, Georgia, a fifteen-year-old student upset over a broken romance opened fire injuring six classmates.

The bloody list could go on ad infinitum. It doesn't take a rocket scientist to figure out what is happening in America. Noah Webster clearly understood what would happen when we remove God from the basis of our government. He penned the following words in 1836:

> The moral principles and concepts contained in the Scriptures ought to form the basis of all our civil constitutions and laws . . . . All the miseries and evils which man may suffer from vice, crime, ambition, injustice, oppression, slavery and war, perceived from their disguising or neglecting the precepts contained in the Bible.[29]

Addressing public school teachers in 1995, Harvard professor Chester M. Pierce told the teachers:

> Every child in America entering school at the age of five is insane because he comes to school with certain allegiances towards our founding fathers, toward his parents, toward a belief in a supernatural being . . . . It is up to you teachers to make all of

---

[29] Noah Webster, HISTORY OF THE UNITED STATES 309-10.

these sick children well by creating the International Children of the Future.[30]

We have reaped what we have sown. God has given us a choice. We can choose His blessings or we can reap the curses. It appears that we are reaping the inevitable results of our rejection of God. It's time to take back America.

---

[30] Berit Kjos, BRAVE NEW SCHOOLS 161.

3

It's Time To Take Back America

We are too late in America's history to remain apathetic or unconcerned. Whether you're a Christian or not, you must admit that America is broken. Something is wrong. The question is how can we fix America. The founders agreed that religious morality and virtue were necessary to good government. Some religion was better than no religion. The founders chose Judeo-Christian religious principles. Though all of the founders were not orthodox Christians, they nevertheless operated from a Judeo-Christian world view. Our public schools inculcated morality and virtue. The governed were self-restrained and therefore needed very little external governmental restraint.

History is a good teacher. If we understand the lessons of our history, we don't have to repeat the mistakes of the past. Comparing the American Revolution to the French Revolution should teach us something. Both revolutions occurred during the same general historical era. Both were concerned with personal liberty. However, the philosophical basis of the two revolutions was fundamentally different. The American Revolution was based upon Judeo-Christian religion, morality and virtue. Spiritual liberty was seen as a prerequisite to physical liberty. The founding fathers believed that external liberty was not possible without a precedent of spiritual liberty.

Alexis deTocqueville was the famous French statesman, historian and social philosopher who toured the United

States in 1831. Documenting his observations of America, deTocqueville stated:

> Upon my arrival in the United States the religious aspect of the country was the first thing that struck my attention; and the longer I stayed there, the more I perceived the great political consequences resulting from this new state of things.

> In France I had almost always seen the spirit of religion and the spirit of freedom marching in opposite directions. But in America I found they were intimately united and that they reigned in common over the same country.[1]

Unlike the American Revolution, the foundation of the French Revolution was based upon human reason and perfection. In contrast to the religious liberty enjoyed in America, the French Revolution suppressed churches and attempted to close them. The churches were used as a means to inculcate human reasoning. In fact, in most dictatorships or communist regimes, churches are the first target. Despotic governments know that in order to lead people like robots, you must kill their spiritual freedom. That's why the former Soviet Union turned traditional churches into museums. This is precisely what occurred during the French Revolution. The result was not liberty but bloodshed and chaos. Since the American Revolution, America has enjoyed only one government, but since the French Revolution, the French have encountered scores of governmental systems.

---

[1]Alexis deTocqueville, DEMOCRACY IN AMERICA 1:319.

The lesson learned from the French and the American Revolutions is that true liberty can only be established if we base our foundation on God and spiritual freedom. When we suppress spiritual freedom and displace God with human rationale, the government structure we create will eventually self-destruct. We can have no personal freedom in the absence of spiritual freedom.

During the early birth of this country, there was a critical time where our founders were at a crossroads. If they chose one way, our country would never have been birthed, and if they chose another, it would birth the most free country on earth. During the early deliberations when the founders gathered to debate what kind of constitution would govern our new society, there were bitter divisions and bickering. The assembly almost deteriorated and broke up, but at that critical moment, Benjamin Franklin stood up in their midst and spoke these now famous words:

> The small progress we have made after four or five weeks close attendance and continual reasonings with each other -- our different sentiments on almost every question, several of the last producing as many nays as ayes, is methinks a melancholy proof of the imperfection of the Human Understanding. We indeed seem to feel our own want of political wisdom, since we have been running about in search of it. We have gone back to ancient history for models of Government, and examined the different forms of those Republics which having been formed with the seeds of their own dissolution now no longer exist. And we have viewed Modern States all around Europe, but find

none in their Constitutions suitable to our circumstances.

In this situation of this Assembly, groping as it were in the dark to find political truth, and scarce able to distinguish it when presented to us, how has it happened, Sir, that we have not hitherto once thought of humbly applying to the Father of lights to illuminate our understandings? In the beginning of the Contest with Great Britain, when we were sensible of danger we had daily prayer in this room for the divine protection. Our prayers, Sir, were heard, and they were graciously answered. All of us who were engaged in the struggle must have observed frequent instances of a Superintending providence in our favor. To that kind providence we owe this happy opportunity of consulting in peace on the means of establishing our future national felicity. And have we now forgotten that powerful friend? Or do we imagine that we no longer need his assistance? I have lived, Sir, a long time, and the longer I live, the more convincing proofs I see of this truth -- that God governs in the affairs of men. And if a sparrow cannot fall to the ground without his notice, is it probable that an empire can rise without his aid? We have been assured, Sir, in the sacred writings, that "except the Lord build the House they labour in vain that build it." I firmly believe this; and I also believe that without his concurring aid we shall succeed in this political building no better than the Builders of Babel: We shall be divided by our little partial local interests; our projects will be confounded, and we ourselves shall become a reproach and bye word down to future ages.[2]

Now that our country has been established and we have come through the early period of bloodshed, have we forgotten our most powerful friend, or do we suppose we no longer need Him? "Except the Lord build the house they labor in vain that build it."[3] As Benjamin Franklin noted, if we do not invoke God in our daily lives and make him the foundation of government, we shall succeed in this political building no better than the builders of Babel. We will be divided by our local partial interests. Our projects will be confounded and we will become a reproach to future generations.

In order to take back America, we must have a spiritual revival and we must become involved in our society. Oftentimes when talking about this subject, people take an either/or approach to the matter. Some people tend toward the pietistic side of things and say that the only thing we can do is pray. Others tend to the political power side of the coin and say that we must enact new laws to reflect our values. The truth of the matter is that we must do both. We must pray and we must become active.

Obviously we are involved in a spiritual battle. The battles and the struggles that we see in the physical realm

---

[2] Benjamin Franklin, Invocation for Prayer at the Constitutional Convention, June 28, 1787, *reprinted in* William Bennett, OUR SACRED HONOR 383-385.

[3] Psalm 127:1.

are simply an outgrowth of the broader spiritual battle going on in the cosmos between Christ and Satan. In the book of Daniel, the prophet had a dream. He was disturbed by the dream and asked God to give him the interpretation. In Chapter 10, verse 4, the angel Gabriel came to Daniel three weeks after he began his prayer for the interpretation of the dream. Gabriel stated to Daniel that God heard his prayer on the very day he prayed and dispensed Gabriel to Daniel to interpret the dream. However, the angel stated that he was delayed for three weeks because he was engaged in a battle against the prince of Persia. In the context of the chapter, the prince of Persia is a spiritual angel over the nation of Persia. Historically, Daniel was a Jewish captive in the nation of Medo-Persia and that country was under siege by the rival nation of Greece. On earth there was a physical battle going on between the nations of Medo-Persia and Greece. The reason the angel Gabriel was delayed is because when he was sent to Daniel who resided in the nation of Greece, the prince of the opposing nation battled Gabriel. Gabriel had to do battle in the spiritual realm so that he could come to Daniel in the physical realm to interpret the dream.

The point of the chapter is that what we see in the physical realm has a counterpart in the spiritual. Obviously we need to be engaged in prayer on behalf of our country. Prayer is a powerful weapon. The Apostle Paul tells us in the book of Ephesians about spiritual warfare:

> For our struggle is not against flesh and blood, but against the rulers, against the authorities, against the powers in this dark world and against the spiritual forces of evil in the heavenly realms.

Therefore put on the full armor of God, so that when the day of evil comes, you may be able to stand your ground, and after you have done everything, to stand. Stand firm then, with the belt of truth buckled around your waist, with the breastplate of righteousness in place, with your feet fitted with the readiness that comes from the gospel of peace. In addition to all this, take up the shield of faith, with which you can extinguish all the flaming arrows of the evil one. Take the helmet of salvation and the sword of the Spirit, which is the word of God. And pray in the Spirit on all occasions with all kinds of prayers and requests. With this in mind, be alert and always keep on praying for all the saints.[4]

There is no question that we must have spiritual revival in America. We can have every just and perfect law, but if our people don't have a life-changing experience, all of the laws will mean nothing. As John Adams once stated, "Our Constitution was made only for a moral and religious people. It is wholly inadequate to the government of any other."[5]

In addition to prayer and a changed life, we must also have a renewed mind. Our laws must reflect our spiritual renewal. The spiritual liberty must produce physical

---

[4] Ephesians 6:12-18.

[5] John Adams, Letter "To the officers of the First Brigade of the Third Division of the Militia of Massachusetts," October 11, 1798, *reprinted in* Bennett, OUR SACRED HONOR 370.

liberty. As the Declaration of Independence states, governments are instituted primarily for the purpose of protecting our God-given, pre-existing unalienable rights. If government must protect these God-given liberties, then government must reflect these liberties in its laws and policies. We therefore must enact laws that reflect our values. This does not mean that we pass legislation requiring everyone to believe in a certain way or attend a certain church. However, all of our laws contain some kind of moral judgment. A law against protecting private property is a moral judgment that people have the right to own private property. Our laws against murder contain a moral judgment that life is sacred and murder is wrong. Every law reflects some kind of moral judgment. Simply because the moral judgment happens to be supported by or is coincident with our religious belief is no reason not to have the law. Christians have been intimidated into silence by anti-religious organizations stating that Christians are imposing their morality when they enter into the political realm. Certainly Christians are imposing their morality, but someone who is not a Christian is also imposing their morality. All laws contain a moral or an amoral basis. All laws are value judgments. Clearly your Christian faith is not a disability. Obviously the founders of this country believed that our Christian liberty was essential to good government. In the absence of our spiritual liberty, our physical liberty will obviously fail.

The history of Christianity in this country is like a pendulum. Christian influences have had their ebb and flow. Our public schools originally taught people how to read solely for the purpose of being able to read the Bible. Our public schools inculcated religious instruction for over two hundred years. It was not until the early 1960's that religious morality and teaching in the public schools was ever questioned or challenged by our judicial system. Booting religion out of our public schools is in fact a recent phenomenon. Why is it that public schools are such a target of religious controversy? The obvious answer is that in order to change the future of America, the easiest and quickest way is to change the minds of our young people. It only takes two generations of school students (just twenty-four years) to have a profound impact on America.

One recent public school history book contains several pages on Marilyn Monroe and a small short paragraph on George Washington. When our school textbooks rewrite American history and erase from that history our Judeo-Christian heritage, the students learn of a different America than our founding fathers knew. When our students are taught moral relativism, it is no wonder why they pick up a gun and shoot another student for no explainable reason. Most of us have been funneled through the public education system. Certainly there are good Christian teachers and students in the public schools. I am not criticizing them, but we must admit that the system is broken.

The public school system in general is a change agent and it teaches certain values. If the values are not religiously based, then the "values" will be wholly secular. Here again, we get back to the difference between the American and French Revolutions. In a religious-based system, there are absolute values. We are taught that we are made in the image of God and have value. We are also taught that others have value and we must respect them. There are transcendent rights and wrongs. A human-based system really doesn't place much value on humanity since humanity is no different than the animal kingdom. There are no transcendent values in a human-based system since these values change over time and vary from one person to the next. Therefore there is no absolute right and wrong in the human-based system. A human-based system is a recipe for chaos.

To take back America, we must not only be involved in the political system but we must also be involved in the educational system. We must run for office. We must vote. We must challenge the idea of the public school monopoly.

We must also become educated about our Judeo-Christian beliefs, values, and our history. If we don't know the basis of our government and the reasons for its creation, then every wind of doctrine or new idea articulated by some eloquent speaker will captivate our mind and change our values. Every time we drive on the road we must know the rules of the road. If you don't know the rules of the road, you won't know how to navigate or how fast to drive.

When the fundamental issue at stake is the ability to share the gospel of Jesus Christ and to change another person's life forever, we must know the rules of our society that either help or hinder us in that endeavor. We must be able to recognize whether these rules or whether the pontifications of those in authority are right or wrong. We must not take legislation at face value but we must challenge these enactments to determine whether they are correct. For example, if you go to a public library and ask permission to use the common meeting room for a religious meeting, do you simply turn away when you see a policy that says the common room can be used for secular but not religious purposes? If you don't know your liberties, you will turn away and think it strange but not challenge the system. However, if you know your liberties and understand that this religious discrimination policy is fundamentally wrong, you will challenge the system. You will try first to change it in an amicable fashion, but if government won't listen to your reasonable claims, then you have the alternative to use the judicial system as a check on government to bring the system back into line. Remember, the purpose of government is to protect your God-given, pre-existing, unalienable rights. To become informed of these liberties, you need to read and educate yourself. Liberty Counsel has a list of resources to equip you.

We must also stand behind those organizations that are making a difference in America. It is amusing that when we take $100.00 to the mall it seems pretty small, but when we think about giving $100.00 to our church or to a non-profit organization, it seems like a large contribution. The founding fathers were willing to sacrifice their lives and their fortunes to preserve our liberty. We must be vigilant to preserve our liberty. You may not be able to enter into a courtroom and may not want to, but there are organizations that battle for your freedom every day. Liberty Counsel is one of those organizations. Litigation is oftentimes a necessary activity to protect our freedoms. It is also an expensive endeavor. On one case that we took to the United States Supreme Court, we had to print a two-volume appendix for the Supreme Court. Special printers have to be used for Supreme Court documents. The printing cost alone that we paid to the printer was almost

$20,000.00. Though the cost of litigation may be high, the cost of surrender is too great to bear.

It is time to take back America. We not only owe it to our founding fathers and ourselves, but we also are obligated to preserve a free America for our children. The task may seem insurmountable. If you are overwhelmed by the prospect, let me remind you of one scene in the Wizard of Oz. You remember when Dorothy and her entourage were nervously walking down the long hallway to see the Wizard. They were intimidated by their surroundings. The booming voice of the Wizard accompanied by puffs of smoke were frightening. Some of the group were tempted to turn back and run. When they were nervously huddled together in fear of their lives, little Toto calmly walked up to the curtain behind which the Wizard sat. He gently tugged on the bottom of the curtain and pulled it back. There sat a spindly old man on a chair speaking into a microphone and pushing buttons to magnify his voice and manipulate the smoke. All of a sudden, the fear that once gripped them vanished. The Wizard was not so big after all.

The ACLU and all other anti-religious groups are like the Wizard. These groups may huff and puff and intimidate the weak at heart, but we must ask God to pull back the curtain so we can see Him standing by our side. We must boldly move forward in confidence. We must take back America.

Appendix A

Deuteronomy 28

1 If you fully obey the LORD your God and carefully follow all his commands I give you today, the LORD your God will set you high above all the nations on earth.

2 All these blessings will come upon you and accompany you if you obey the LORD your God:

3 You will be blessed in the city and blessed in the country.

4 The fruit of your womb will be blessed, and the crops of your land and the young of your livestock--the calves of your herds and the lambs of your flocks.

5 Your basket and your kneading trough will be blessed.

6 You will be blessed when you come in and blessed when you go out.

7 The LORD will grant that the enemies who rise up against you will be defeated before you. They will come at you from one direction but flee from you in seven.

8 The LORD will send a blessing on your barns and on everything you put your hand to. The LORD your God will bless you in the land he is giving you.

9 The LORD will establish you as his holy people, as he promised you on oath, if you keep the commands of the LORD your God and walk in his ways.

10 Then all the peoples on earth will see that you are called by the name of the LORD, and they will fear you.

11 The LORD will grant you abundant prosperity--in the fruit of your womb, the young of your livestock and the crops of your ground--in the land he swore to your forefathers to give you.

12 The LORD will open the heavens, the storehouse of his bounty, to send rain on your land in season and to bless all

the work of your hands. You will lend to many nations but will borrow from none.

13 The LORD will make you the head, not the tail. If you pay attention to the commands of the LORD your God that I give you this day and carefully follow them, you will always be at the top, never at the bottom.

14 Do not turn aside from any of the commands I give you today, to the right or to the left, following other gods and serving them.

15 However, if you do not obey the LORD your God and do not carefully follow all his commands and decrees I am giving you today, all these curses will come upon you and overtake you:

16 You will be cursed in the city and cursed in the country.

17 Your basket and your kneading trough will be cursed.

18 The fruit of your womb will be cursed, and the crops of your land, and the calves of your herds and the lambs of your flocks.

19 You will be cursed when you come in and cursed when you go out.

20 The LORD will send on you curses, confusion and rebuke in everything you put your hand to, until you are destroyed and come to sudden ruin because of the evil you have done in forsaking him.

21 The LORD will plague you with diseases until he has destroyed you from the land you are entering to possess.

22 The LORD will strike you with wasting disease, with fever and inflammation, with scorching heat and drought, with blight and mildew, which will plague you until you perish.

23 The sky over your head will be bronze, the ground beneath you iron.

24 The LORD will turn the rain of your country into dust and powder; it will come down from the skies until you are destroyed.

25 The LORD will cause you to be defeated before your enemies. You will come at them from one direction but flee from them in seven, and you will become a thing of horror to all the kingdoms on earth.

26 Your carcasses will be food for all the birds of the air and the beasts of the earth, and there will be no one to frighten them away.

27 The LORD will afflict you with the boils of Egypt and with tumors, festering sores and the itch, from which you cannot be cured.

28 The LORD will afflict you with madness, blindness and confusion of mind.

29 At midday you will grope about like a blind man in the dark. You will be unsuccessful in everything you do; day after day you will be oppressed and robbed, with no one to rescue you.

30 You will be pledged to be married to a woman, but another will take her and ravish her. You will build a house, but you will not live in it. You will plant a vineyard, but you will not even begin to enjoy its fruit.

31 Your ox will be slaughtered before your eyes, but you will eat none of it. Your donkey will be forcibly taken from you and will not be returned. Your sheep will be given to your enemies, and no one will rescue them.

32 Your sons and daughters will be given to another nation, and you will wear out your eyes watching for them day after day, powerless to lift a hand.

33 A people that you do not know will eat what your land and labor produce, and you will have nothing but cruel oppression all your days.

34 The sights you see will drive you mad.

35 The LORD will afflict your knees and legs with painful boils that cannot be cured, spreading from the soles of your feet to the top of your head.

36 The LORD will drive you and the king you set over you to a nation unknown to you or your fathers. There you will worship other gods, gods of wood and stone.

37 You will become a thing of horror and an object of scorn and ridicule to all the nations where the LORD will drive you.

38 You will sow much seed in the field but you will harvest little, because locusts will devour it.

39 You will plant vineyards and cultivate them but you will not drink the wine or gather the grapes, because worms will eat them.

40 You will have olive trees throughout your country but you will not use the oil, because the olives will drop off.

41 You will have sons and daughters but you will not keep them, because they will go into captivity.

42 Swarms of locusts will take over all your trees and the crops of your land.

43 The alien who lives among you will rise above you higher and higher, but you will sink lower and lower.

44 He will lend to you, but you will not lend to him. He will be the head, but you will be the tail.

45 All these curses will come upon you. They will pursue you and overtake you until you are destroyed, because you did not obey the LORD your God and observe the commands and decrees he gave you.

46 They will be a sign and a wonder to you and your descendants forever.

47 Because you did not serve the LORD your God joyfully and gladly in the time of prosperity,

48 therefore in hunger and thirst, in nakedness and dire poverty, you will serve the enemies the LORD sends against you. He will put an iron yoke on your neck until he has destroyed you.

49 The LORD will bring a nation against you from far away, from the ends of the earth, like an eagle swooping down, a nation whose language you will not understand,

50 a fierce-looking nation without respect for the old or pity for the young.

51 They will devour the young of your livestock and the crops of your land until you are destroyed. They will leave you no grain, new wine or oil, nor any calves of your herds or lambs of your flocks until you are ruined.

52 They will lay siege to all the cities throughout your land until the high fortified walls in which you trust fall down. They will besiege all the cities throughout the land the LORD your God is giving you.

53 Because of the suffering that your enemy will inflict on you during the siege, you will eat the fruit of the womb, the flesh of the sons and daughters the LORD your God has given you.

54 Even the most gentle and sensitive man among you will have no compassion on his own brother or the wife he loves or his surviving children,

55 and he will not give to one of them any of the flesh of his children that he is eating. It will be all he has left because of the suffering your enemy will inflict on you during the siege of all your cities.

56   The most gentle and sensitive woman among you--so sensitive and gentle that she would not venture to touch the ground with the sole of her foot--will begrudge the husband she loves and her own son or daughter

57 the afterbirth from her womb and the children she bears. For she intends to eat them secretly during the siege and in the distress that your enemy will inflict on you in your cities.

58 If you do not carefully follow all the words of this law, which are written in this book, and do not revere this glorious and awesome name--the LORD your God--

59   the LORD will send fearful plagues on you and your descendants, harsh and prolonged disasters, and severe and lingering illnesses.

60 He will bring upon you all the diseases of Egypt that you dreaded, and they will cling to you.

61   The LORD will also bring on you every kind of sickness and disaster not recorded in this Book of the Law, until you are destroyed.

62 You who were as numerous as the stars in the sky will be left but few in number, because you did not obey the LORD your God.

63 Just as it pleased the LORD to make you prosper and increase in number, so it will please him to ruin and destroy you. You will be uprooted from the land you are entering to possess.

64   Then the LORD will scatter you among all nations, from one end of the earth to the other. There you will worship other gods--gods of wood and stone, which neither you nor your fathers have known.

65 Among those nations you will find no repose, no resting place for the sole of your foot. There the LORD will give

you an anxious mind, eyes weary with longing, and a despairing heart.

66 You will live in constant suspense, filled with dread both night and day, never sure of your life.

67 In the morning you will say, "If only it were evening!" and in the evening, "If only it were morning!"--because of the terror that will fill your hearts and the sights that your eyes will see.

68 The LORD will send you back in ships to Egypt on a journey I said you should never make again. There you will offer yourselves for sale to your enemies as male and female slaves, but no one will buy you.[6]

---

[6] Scripture taken from the HOLY BIBLE, NEW INTERNATIONAL VERSION. Copyright © 1973, 1978, 1984 by International Bible Society. Used by permission.

Appendix B

Declaration of Independence

In Congress, July 4, 1776
The Unanimous Declaration of the Thirteen United States of America

When in the Course of human events it becomes necessary for one people to dissolve the political bands which have connected them with another, and to assume among the Powers of the earth, the separate and equal station to which the Laws of Nature and of Nature's God entitle them, a decent respect to the opinions of mankind requires that they should declare the causes which impel them to the separation.

We hold these truths to be self-evident, that all men are created equal, that they are endowed by their Creator with certain unalienable Rights, that among these are Life, Liberty and the pursuit of Happiness. That to secure these rights, Governments are instituted among Men, deriving their just powers from the consent of the governed, That whenever any Form of Government becomes destructive of these ends, it is the Right of the People to alter or to abolish it, and to institute new Government, laying its foundation on such principles and organizing its powers in such form, as to them shall seem most likely to effect their Safety and Happiness. Prudence, indeed, will dictate that Governments long established should not be changed for light and transient causes; and accordingly all experience hath shown, that mankind are more disposed to suffer, while evils are sufferable, than to right themselves by abolishing the forms to which they are accustomed. But when a long train of abuses and usurpations, pursuing invariably the same Object evinces a design to reduce them under absolute Despotism, it is their right, it is their duty, to throw off such Government, and to provide new Guards for their future security.--Such has been the patient sufferance of these Colonies; and such is now the necessity which constrains them to alter their former Systems of Government. The history of the present King of Great Britain is a history of repeated injuries and usurpations, all having in direct object the establishment of an absolute Tyranny over these States. To prove this, let Facts be submitted to a candid world.

He has refused his Assent to Laws, the most wholesome and necessary for the public good.

He has forbidden his Governors to pass Laws of immediate and pressing importance, unless suspended in their operation till his Assent should be obtained; and when so suspended, he has utterly neglected to attend to them.

He has refused to pass other Laws for the accommodation of large districts of people, unless those people would relinquish the right of Representation in the Legislature, a right inestimable to them and formidable to tyrants only.

He has called together legislative bodies at places unusual, uncomfortable, and distant from the depository of their Public Records, for the sole purpose of fatiguing them into compliance with his measures.

He has dissolved Representative Houses repeatedly, for opposing with manly firmness his invasions on the rights of the people.

He has refused for a long time, after such dissolutions, to cause others to be elected; whereby the Legislative Powers, incapable of Annihilation, have returned to the People at large for their exercise; the State remaining in the mean time exposed to all the dangers of invasion from without, and convulsions within.

He has endeavored to prevent the population of these States; for that purpose obstructing the Laws for Naturalization of Foreigners; refusing to pass others to encourage their migration hither, and raising the conditions of new Appropriations of Lands.

He has obstructed the Administration of Justice, by refusing his Assent to Laws for establishing Judiciary Powers.

He has made Judges dependent on his Will alone, for the tenure of their offices, and the amount and payment of their salaries.

He has erected a multitude of New Offices, and sent hither swarms of Officers to harass our People, and eat out their substance.

He has kept among us, in times of peace, Standing Armies without the Consent of our Legislature.

He has affected to render the Military independent of and superior to the Civil Power.

He has combined with others to subject us to a jurisdiction foreign to our constitution, and unacknowledged by our laws; giving his Assent to their acts of pretended Legislation:

For quartering large bodies of armed troops among us:

For protecting them, by a mock Trial, from Punishment for any Murders which they should commit on the Inhabitants of these States:

For cutting off our Trade with all parts of the world:

For imposing taxes on us without our Consent:

For depriving us in many cases, of the benefits of Trial by Jury:

For transporting us beyond Seas to be tried for pretended offenses:

For abolishing the free System of English Laws in a neighboring Province, establishing therein an Arbitrary government, and enlarging its Boundaries so as to render it at once an example and fit instrument for introducing the same absolute rule into these Colonies:

For taking away our Charters, abolishing our most valuable Laws, and altering fundamentally the Forms of our Government:

For suspending our own Legislature, and declaring themselves invested with Power to legislate for us in all cases whatsoever.

He has abdicated Government here, by declaring us out of his Protection and waging War against us.

He has plundered our seas, ravaged our Coasts, burnt our towns, and destroyed the lives of our people.

He is at this time transporting large armies of foreign mercenaries to compleat the works of death, desolation and tyranny, already begun with circumstances of Cruelty & perfidy scarcely paralleled in the most barbarous ages, and totally unworthy the Head of a civilized nation.

He has constrained our fellow Citizens taken Captive on the high Seas to bear Arms against their Country, to become the executioners of their friends and Brethren, or to fall themselves by their Hands.

He has excited domestic insurrections amongst us, and has endeavored to bring on the inhabitants of our frontiers, the merciless Indian Savages, whose known rule of warfare, is an undistinguished destruction of all ages, sexes and conditions.

In every stage of these Oppressions We have Petitioned for Redress in the most humble terms: Our repeated Petitions have been answered only by repeated injury. A Prince, whose character is thus marked by every act which may define a Tyrant, is unfit to be the ruler of a free People.

Nor have We been wanting in attention to our British brethren.   We have warned them from time to time of attempts by their legislature to extend an unwarrantable jurisdiction over us.   We have reminded them of the circumstances of our emigration and settlement here. We have appealed to their native justice and magnanimity, and we have conjured them by the ties of our common kindred to disavow these usurpations, which, would inevitably interrupt our connections and correspondence. They too have been deaf to the voice of justice and consanguinity. We must, therefore, acquiesce in the necessity, which denounces our Separation, and hold them, as we hold the rest of mankind, Enemies in War, in Peace Friends.

We, therefore, the Representatives of the United States of America, in General Congress, Assembled, appealing to the Supreme Judge of the world for the rectitude of our intentions, do, in the Name, and by Authority of the good People of these Colonies, solemnly publish and declare, That these United Colonies are, and of Right ought to be Free and Independent States; that they are Absolved from all Allegiance to the British Crown, and that all political connection between them and the State of Great Britain, is and ought to be totally dissolved;   and that as Free and Independent States, they have full Power to levy War, conclude Peace, contract Alliances, establish Commerce, and to do all other Acts and Things which Independent States may of right do. And for the support of this Declaration, with a firm reliance on the Protection of Divine Providence, we mutually pledge to each other our Lives, our Fortunes and our sacred Honor.

Connecticut:	Roger Sherman
	William Williams
	Samuel Huntington
	Oliver Wolcott
Delaware:	Caesar Rodney
	Thomas McKean
	George Read
Georgia:	Button Gwinnett
	George Walton
	Lyman Hall
Maryland:	Samuel Chase
	Thomas Stone
	William Paca
	Charles Carroll of Carrollton
Massachusetts:	John Hancock
	Samuel Adams
	Robert Treat Paine
	John Adams
	Elbridge Gerry
New Hampshire:	Josiah Bartlett
	Matthew Thornton
	William Whipple
New Jersey:	Richard Stockton
	John Hart
	John Witherspoon

Abraham Clark
Francis Hopkinson
New York: William Floyd
Francis Lewis
Philip Livingston
Lewis Morris
North Carolina: William Hooper
John Penn
Joseph Hewes
Pennsylvania: Robert Morris
James Smith
Benjamin Rush
George Taylor
Benjamin Franklin
James Wilson
John Morton
George Ross
George Clymer
Rhode Island: Stephen Hopkins
William Ellery
South Carolina: Edward Rutledge
Thomas Lynch, Jr.
Thomas Heyward, Jr.
Arthur Middleton
Virginia: George Wythe
Thomas Nelson, Jr.
Richard Henry Lee
Francis Lightfoot Lee
Thomas Jefferson
Benjamin Harrison
Carter Braxton

Appendix C

Eighth Grade Final Exam

Contained below is a final exam given to eighth grade students in Salina, Kansas, in 1895. The exam is taken from the original document on file at the Smoky Valley Genealogical Society and Library in Salina, Kansas, and reprinted by the *Salina Journal* on July 7, 2000. *See* http://www.saljournal.com.

8th Grade Final Exam: Salina, Kansas - 1895

Grammar (Time, 1 hour)
1. Give nine rules for the use of Capital Letters.
2. Name the Parts of Speech and define those that have no modifications.
3. Define Verse, Stanza and Paragraph.
4. What are the Principal Parts of a verb? Give Principal Parts of do, lie, lay and run.
5. Define Case. Illustrate each Case.
6. What is Punctuation? Give rules for principal marks of Punctuation.
7. Write a composition of about 150 words and show therein that you understand the practical use of the rules of grammar.

Arithmetic (Time, 1½ hours)
1. Name and define the Fundamental Rules of Arithmetic.
2. A wagon box is 2 feet deep, 10 feet long, and 3 feet wide. How many bushels of wheat will it hold?
3. If a load of wheat weighs 3,942 lbs., what is it worth at 50 cts. per bu., deducting 1,050 lbs. for tare?

4. District No. 33 has a valuation of $35,000. What is the necessary
    levy to carry on a school seven months at $50 per month, and have $104 for incidentals?
5. Find the cost of 6,720 lbs. coal at $6.00 per ton.
6. Find the interest of $512.60 for 8 months and 18 days at 7 percent.
7. What is the cost of 40 boards 12 inches wide and 16 feet long at $20 per inch?
8. Find the bank discount on $300 for 90 days (no grace) at 10 percent.
9. What is the cost of a square farm at $15 per acre, the distance around which is 640 rods?
10. Write a Bank Check, a Promissory Note, and a Receipt.

U.S. History (Time, 45 minutes)
1. Give the epochs into which U.S. History is divided.
2. Give an account of the discovery of America by Columbus.
3. Relate the causes and results of the Revolutionary War.
4. Show the territorial growth of the United States.
5. Tell what you can of the history of Kansas.
6. Describe three of the most prominent battles of the Rebellion.
7. Who were the following: Morse, Whitney, Fulton, Bell, Lincoln, Penn, and Howe?
8. Name events connected with the following dates: 1607, 1620, 1800, 1849, and 1865.

Orthography (Time, 1 hour)
1. What is meant by the following: Alphabet, phonetic, orthography, etymology, syllabication?

2. What are elementary sounds? How classified?
3. What are the following, and give examples of each: Trigraph, subvocals, diphthong, cognate letters, linguals?
4. Give four substitutes for caret "u".
5. Give two rules for spelling words with final "e". Name two exceptions under each rule.
6. Give two uses of silent letters in spelling. Illustrate each.
7. Define the following prefixes and use in connection with a word: Bi, dis, mis, pre, semi, post, non, inter, mono, super.
8. Mark diacritically and divide into syllables the following, and name the sign that indicates the sound: Card, ball, mercy, sir, odd, cell, rise, blood, fare, last.
9. Use the following correctly in sentences: cite, site, sight, fane, fain, feign, vane, vain, vein, raze, raise, rays.
10. Write 10 words frequently mispronounced and indicate pronunciation by use of diacritical marks and by syllabication.

Geography (Time, 1 hour)
1. What is climate? Upon what does climate depend?
2. How do you account for the extremes of climate in Kansas?
3. Of what use are rivers? Of what use is the ocean?
4. Describe the mountains of North America.
5. Name and describe the following: Monrovia, Odessa, Denver, Manitoba, Hecla, Yukon, St. Helena, Juan Fermandez, Aspinwall and Orinoco.
6. Name and locate the principal trade centers of the U.S.

7. Name all the republics of Europe and give capital of each.
8. Why is the Atlantic Coast colder than the Pacific in the same latitude?
9. Describe the process by which the water of the ocean returns to the sources of rivers.
10. Describe the movements of the earth. Give inclination of the earth.

About the Author

Mathew D. Staver is an attorney who specializes in free speech and religious liberty constitutional law. He is board certified by the Florida Bar in Appellate Practice and Workers' Compensation.

In 1989, Mat became founder and president of Liberty Counsel, a civil liberties education and legal defense organization established to preserve religious freedom. Based in Orlando, Florida, Liberty Counsel provides education and legal defense throughout the nation. As president, Mr. Staver has produced many informative brochures, books, and articles on religious liberty and free speech issues. He is editor of *The Liberator*, a monthly newsletter devoted to religious liberty, free speech and pro-family topics. He hosts *Freedom's Call*, a two minute daily radio commentary, and *Faith and Freedom*, a fifteen minute daily radio program, both of which are dedicated to religious freedom, free speech and pro-family issues. Mat is a frequent guest on radio and television programs throughout the country. His religious liberty commentary is regularly seen on the nationally televised program, *Listen America*.

Mat has authored a number of books including, *Faith and Freedom; Religion and the Future of America; Religious Expression in Public Schools; Judicial Tyranny; Political Activity of Nonprofit Organizations; Same-sex Marriage;* and *Union Membership and its Constitutional Implications*. He has also authored several law review articles along with hundreds of other articles and brochures on constitutional law. Mat writes a monthly column for the *National Liberty Journal*.

In addition to receiving a doctorate of law degree, Mat graduated *summa cum laude* with a Master of Arts degree in Religion. He reads Greek, Hebrew, Aramaic, and Syriac. While pursuing graduate study, he was an honorary guest lecturer at the American Society of Oriental Research at the University of Illinois. Prior to entering law school, Mat served as a pastor in the state of Kentucky.

He has numerous legal opinions credited to his work and has argued before the United States Supreme Court.

About Liberty Counsel

Liberty Counsel is a nonprofit civil liberties education and legal defense organization established to preserve religious freedom. Founded in 1989 by president and general counsel, Mathew D. Staver, Liberty Counsel accomplishes its purpose in a two-fold manner: through education and legal defense.

Liberty Counsel produces many aids to educate in matters of religious liberty. *The Liberator* is a monthly newsletter reviewing various religious liberty, free speech, and pro-family issues throughout the nation. The *Liberty Alert* is Liberty Counsel's periodic email newsletter. *Freedom's Call* is a two-minute daily radio program produced by Liberty Counsel providing education in First Amendment religious liberties. *Faith and Freedom* is a fifteen minute daily radio program dedicated to religious liberty, free speech and pro-family matters. Mat is a regular guest commentator on the nationally televised program called *Listen America*. Many of these resources may be obtained on our web site which is listed below.

Liberty Counsel has produced many brochures, books, tapes and articles outlining various aspects of religious liberty. Most of the cases in which Liberty Counsel is involved resolve through education, either by a telephone call, informative literature, or letters. Many individuals and public officials are ignorant and misinformed regarding the First Amendment. Religious and free speech rights are often restricted or lost because of ignorance.

Unfortunately, education will not solve all religious liberty issues. Some individuals are hostile and bigoted toward religion. If education does not resolve the issue, Liberty Counsel aggressively fights for religious liberty in the courtroom. Liberty Counsel represents individuals whose religious liberties are infringed, and defends entities against those trying to restrict religious liberty. Liberty Counsel attorneys frequently argue cases throughout the country, including the United States Supreme Court.

Liberty Counsel is a nonprofit tax-exempt corporation dependent upon public financial support. Contributions to Liberty Counsel are tax-deductible. For information about Liberty Counsel, or to make tax-deductible contributions, please write or call:

Liberty Counsel
Post Office Box 540774
Orlando, Florida 32854
(407) 875-2100
(800) 671-1776
(407) 875-0770 Fax
www.lc.org Internet Home Page
liberty@lc.org Internet Email